## THE LONG AND SHORT OF IT

Researched and Collated by Sharron Halstead

Copyright © 2018 by Sharron Halstead
Petitepeds® is a registered trademark of Sharron Halstead
All rights reserved, including the right to reproduce this book or portions thereof in any form whatsoever. Affiliate links may be used, which is at not cost to you.

**ISBN:** 978-0-6451981-0-2

### Credits
Cover graphics, book illustrations and Graphic Design by Karen Hue
Bbook creation by Luca Funari, lucafunari@hotmail.com
Author and images: Luisa Kearney, ©OnlinePersonalStylist.com,
Sharron Halstead © PetitePeds

### Contact
Email: sales@petitepeds.com.au
Website AU: www.petitepeds.com.au
Website US: www.petitepeds.co

Melbourne, Australia

### Cataloguing
National Library of Australia Cataloguing-in Publication Date
Sharon Halstead's Petite Fashion, the Long and Short of It Fashion

**INTRODUCTION** The Long and Short of it

# Petite Fashion

I HAVE A DREAM... a dream to help Petite ladies!

# Welcome

The aim of this book is to provide you with numerous tips (sourced, thoroughly researched and then compiled into one easy to read, direct and explicit beautiful book). I am confident it contains quality content to assist all you beautiful petite ladies out there who struggle with dressing your petite frames and feet.

Now in business for a few years, I have heard all the stories of woe and frustration from my petite customers, not just about shoes but clothing and fashion in general. It has been my catch cry that "Dressing a petite lady is different to dressing an average woman, period."

With a firm interest in being the authority on anything petite, I decided to invest in creating a book to dress the unique petite frame, and combined with a qualified fashion stylist so that we could assist our customers. This book is a culmination of all the research, sourced from qualified stylists, customer feedback and good old-fashioned trial and error, into this very unique E-book targeted at petite ladies. As the saying goes, "necessity is the mother of invention" so it was out of a dire need for change that this e-book was born.

targeted at petite ladies. As the saying goes, "necessity is the mother of invention" so it was out of a dire need for change that this e-book was born.

Remember this book is essentially a reference book, not to be digested in one sitting, but rather to be referred to whenever you have a fashion dilemma or want to know what goes with what, what will suit your body shape or face shape or skin colour or what accessory to match for your height etc.

I would love to get any feedback so please feel free to contact me with comments, questions or suggestions at sales@petitepeds.com.au.

*Yours Fashionably*

Sharron Halstead
Founder, Petitepeds

# Contents

| | | |
|---|---|---|
| **CHAPTER 1** | Petite Women – what is petite? | 9 |
| **CHAPTER 2** | Do's and Don'ts | 16 |
| **CHAPTER 3** | How to create the perfect capsule wardrobe for petit ladies/wardrobe essentials | 23 |
| **CHAPTER 4** | A mini masterclass on choosing shoes | 29 |
| **CHAPTER 5** | Dressing for your skin tone | 38 |
| **CHAPTER 6** | Using colour to dress for your body shape | 46 |
| **CHAPTER 7** | Creating curves through clothing | 52 |
| **CHAPTER 8** | Balancing out your body proportions | 58 |
| **CHAPTER 9** | Bra fittings (cups and sizes for petites), shapewear, underwear, swim suits | 79 |

| CHAPTER 10 | Using jewellery to balance your body proportions.. | 89 |
| --- | --- | --- |
| CHAPTER 11 | Using other accessories to dress............................ | 92 |
| | Hats................................................................. | 94 |
| | Scarves............................................................ | 96 |
| | Glasses............................................................ | 96 |
| | Handbags........................................................ | 99 |
| CHAPTER 12 | How to dress to suit your age............................... | 103 |
| CHAPTER 13 | What is Style and how to achieve it?................... | 109 |
| CHAPTER 14 | What Not to Wear................................................ | 117 |
| CHAPTER 15 | A Look-book of Ideal Clothing............................. | 125 |
| CHAPTER 16 | Different Body Shapes........................................ | 140 |
| | Apple Shapes................................................. | 142 |
| | What is an Apple Shape?............................... | 142 |
| | Ideal Looks for Apple Shape – Day, Night and Skirts and Dresses................ | 148 |

Pear Shape .................................................................. 150
What is Pear Shape? ..................................................... 150
Ideal Looks for Pear Shape – Day,
Night and Skirts and Dresses ....................................... 157
Hourglass Shapes ......................................................... 159
What is an Hourglass Shape? ..................................... 159
Ideal Looks Hour-Glass shape – Day,
Night and Skirts and Dresses ....................................... 164
Straight Shapes ............................................................. 165
What is a Straight Body Shape? .................................. 165
Ideal Looks for Straight Shapes – Day,
Night and Skirts and Dresses ....................................... 171

**CHAPTER 17** Size Guide to Petite Sizes ................................ 174
How to Measure Your Foot ........................................... 180

**BIOGRAPHY** ................................................................... 181
**BONUS SECTION** ........................................................... 184
**REVIEW SECTION** ......................................................... 185

**CHAPTER 1**

# Petite Woman

What is petite?
- Petite is a size determined by nothing more than height

The definition of

*Petite is*

**adjective:**
petite (of a woman) attractively small and dainty. "she was petite and vivacious"

**synonyms:**
small, dainty, diminutive, slight, little, tiny, elfin, delicate, small-boned;

# *It is true*

that many petite women have smaller frames and bone structure than non-petite women however, this doesn't mean that all women have delicate face shapes, tiny waists or boyish figures. The standard height of a woman classed as petite is 5 foot 3 or under. Naturally, a woman of 4 ft 11 is going to be significantly shorter and different in shape and body proportions that a woman of 5 ft 3. This is why you need to understand the many aspects of petite dressing.

> On the plus side, petite women can enjoy the luxury of being taller or shorter at any time they choose with the help of a great pair of heels.

There are many advantages to being a petite lady of heels.

for example:

- Petite women can get away with wearing a greater range of styles and patterns

- Bright colours and different patterns and prints look fabulous on petite women

- It is easier for a petite lady to make herself look curvier, slimmer, taller, younger than her taller counterparts, through the use of clothing.

- Shopping in the sales can (sometimes) be a huge success because we do not share the nation's average shoe and dress size that everybody else seems to be fighting over!

There are four main body shape types:
(we will cover them in more detail throughout this book.)

Apple = you are widest around the tops of your arms, your bust and your waist but are narrower from your hips and below.

Pear = Your widest point is your hips/bottom and thighs – but have a slim, narrow torso.

Straight = Your hips, waist and shoulders all appear the same width and overall, you have a very straight, balanced figure that may appear boyish or athletic.

Hourglass = Your shoulders and bust are approximately the same width as your hips but your waist is around 10 inches smaller. You may also have very slim ankles and wrists.

The key to dressing well as a petite lady is understanding your body shape and learning how to dress for your own individual body shape, because as we have already established – being petite is not a one size fits all types of body shape.
of heels.

*In order to find* clothing and footwear that suit your height and shape, it is best to make an effort to shop in the petite ranges in stores. It's also very important to pay attention to the type of body shape you have when shopping, as few people actually do this and this is one of the main reasons why all women struggle to find clothing that suits them and that flatters them!

## CHAPTER 2
# Do's and Don'ts

Common misconceptions about

## *Petite shapes*

There are many misconceptions about the petite figure. Unlike what you may think, petite body shapes do not have to be any of the following:

- "Skinny"
- Underweight
- Petite is a "body shape"
- Petite women are a "one size fits all" kind of community

Another common misconception about petite ladies is that they have a boyish figure and are very thin, but this is not always the case. It's true that usually petite women have smaller frames, which means that their hips and shoulders are narrower than their taller counterparts but some of the most admired and famous hourglass figures belong to petite ladies. Petite ladies do not lack femininity; just merely lack a little height!

> You would be surprised at just how many shorter ladies there are out there, especially if you are comparing yourself to those on the red carpet

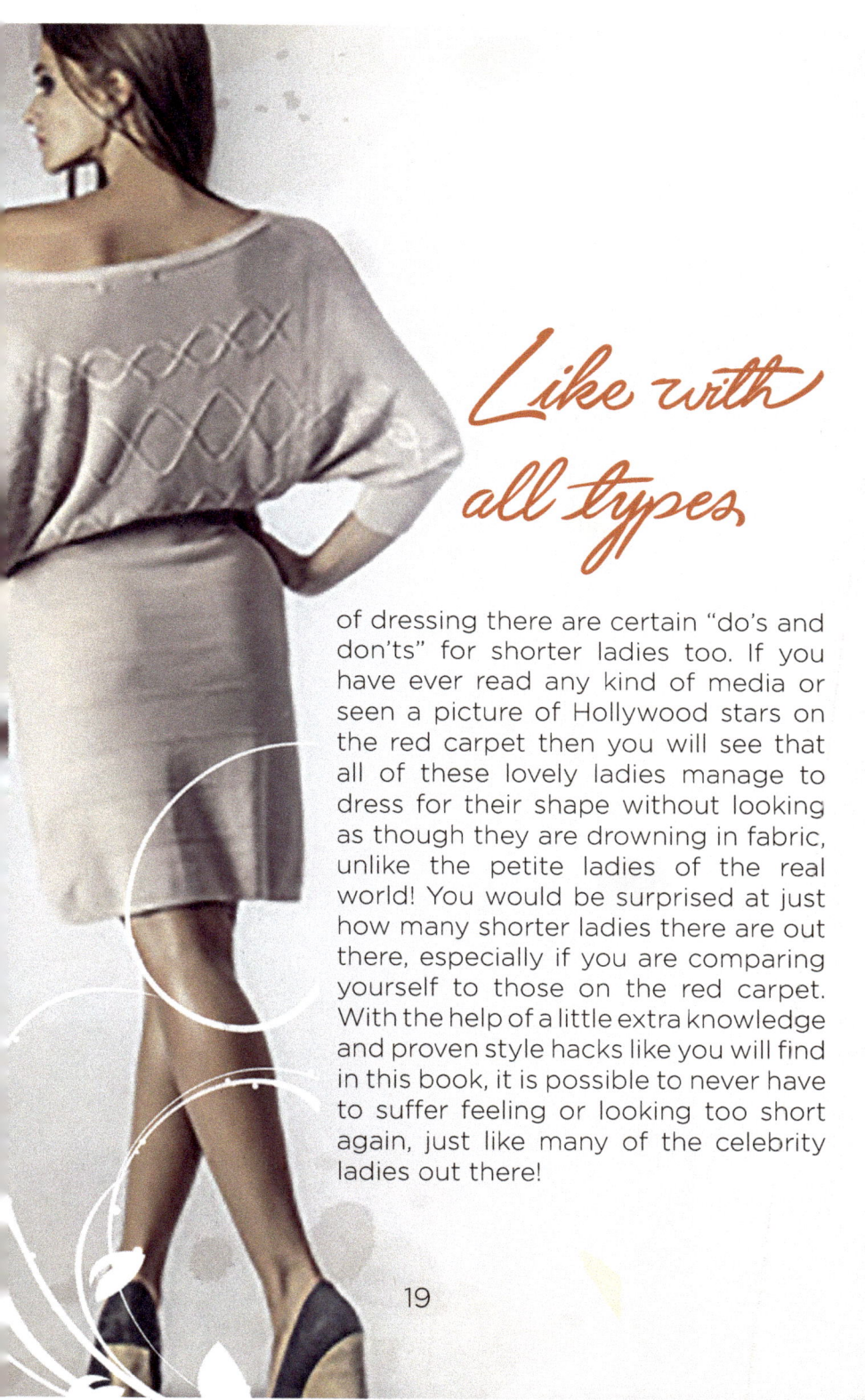

# Like with all types

of dressing there are certain "do's and don'ts" for shorter ladies too. If you have ever read any kind of media or seen a picture of Hollywood stars on the red carpet then you will see that all of these lovely ladies manage to dress for their shape without looking as though they are drowning in fabric, unlike the petite ladies of the real world! You would be surprised at just how many shorter ladies there are out there, especially if you are comparing yourself to those on the red carpet. With the help of a little extra knowledge and proven style hacks like you will find in this book, it is possible to never have to suffer feeling or looking too short again, just like many of the celebrity ladies out there!

# Don't

- Shop in petite ranges to "cheat" your way to tailored fits.

- If you cannot find petite ranges in your nearby clothing stores then hunt out tailor made options.

- In some cases finding decent fitting petite clothing can be a challenge. Rather than buying large quantities of clothing, track down tailor made alternatives and if you have to, invest in a few tailored pieces rather than lots of poor fitting clothing.

- In trousers, straight leg varieties are your best friend. These are the one style that will suit you no matter what your body shape is.

- If possible, match the colour of your footwear to your trousers/bottoms, as this will create the illusion of longer, leaner legs.

- Wear colours from a similar palette, which will complement each other and which will not create a huge contrast. This will make you appear taller, whereas block colours will make you appear shorter.

> Here is a list of all the things you should do and all of the things you shouldn't do when dressing your delicate shape.

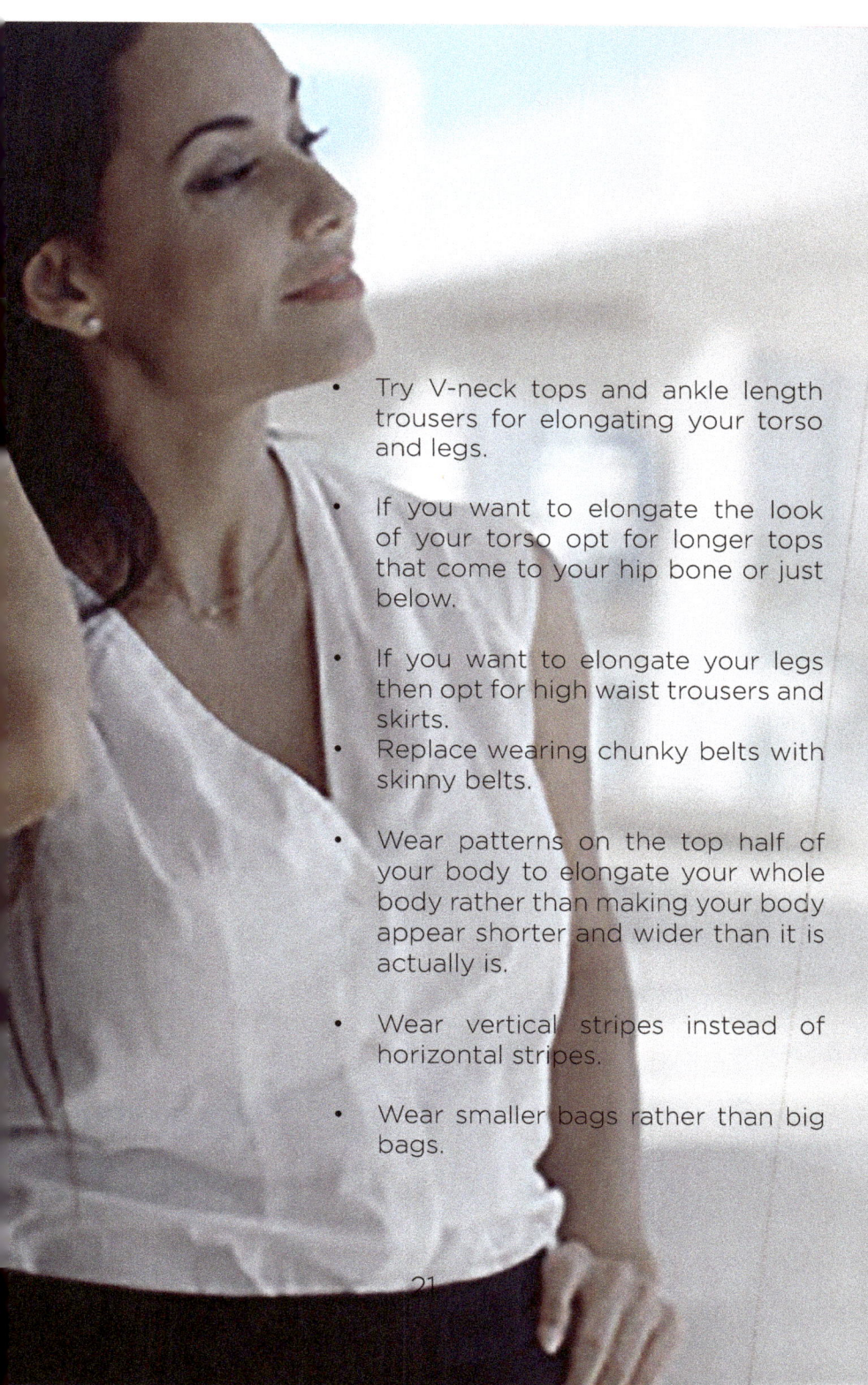

- Try V-neck tops and ankle length trousers for elongating your torso and legs.

- If you want to elongate the look of your torso opt for longer tops that come to your hip bone or just below.

- If you want to elongate your legs then opt for high waist trousers and skirts.
- Replace wearing chunky belts with skinny belts.

- Wear patterns on the top half of your body to elongate your whole body rather than making your body appear shorter and wider than it is actually is.

- Wear vertical stripes instead of horizontal stripes.

- Wear smaller bags rather than big bags.

# Dont's

- Wearing chunky belts will make you appear shorter than what you are.
- Avoid horizontal stripes which will make you appear shorter and wider.
- Try to avoid larger handbags.
- Don't wear ankle straps on shoes.
- Make sure that your boots do not exceed knee length.
- Don't wear baggy tops and bottoms.
- Don't shop in the kids section.
- Don't go against your natural body shape when dressing and shopping, it will prove a waste of money and time.
- Don't choose bottoms that have an obvious mixture of colour, try to opt for one colour on your bottoms.
- Don't team tunics with leggings and skinny jeans, as this will make your legs look extremely short!
- Don't wear skirts or leggings that come to anywhere between your knee and ankle, opt for leggings and skirts that end either at your knee or ankles but not in between.
- Avoid oversized jewellery and accessories.

**CHAPTER 3**

# How to create

the perfect capsule wardrobe for petite ladies/ wardrobe essentials

# What is a Capsule Wardrobe?

A capsule wardrobe is a neat and concise wardrobe, full of garments and accessories that suit one another, that can be thrown together with ease to create perfect outfits and also, it must contain items that you will wear regularly. In other words, a capsule wardrobe is a wardrobe full of style staples. One of the biggest mistakes that many women make when dressing, as well as when shopping for clothes, is that they jump into the deep end first and opt for bright colours and daring fits. You must start with the basics, wear them, and gradually build upon them using only items that suit your body shape.

> Start with the basics, wear them, and gradually buil upon them using only itmes that suit your body shape.

# the best way

to build a wardrobe that will serve as both useful and fun to work with is to start with the basics and built on what you already have. Ideally, every wardrobe should have a certain number of items from which you will easily be able to form stylish yet fuss free outfits without wasting hours doing so. Of course, feel free to eliminate any items on this list that you just would not wear, but the basics you need to create your perfect capsule wardrobe are:

- Black vest top
- White vest top
- Black t-shirt
- White t-shirt
- Long sleeve black top
- Long sleeve white top
- White blouse
- A basic button up cardigan
- A large scarf/shawl
- A stylish clutch bag
- A big buckle belt
- A cream trench coat
- A black leather jacket
- Black trousers
- Indigo Jeans

- Faded Jeans
- White Jeans
- A well-fitted denim jacket
- A fitted blazer jacket
- A "it fits everything" handbag
- A tailored handbag
- Hoodie type sweatshirt
- Black dress
- A pair of classic stiletto heels
- Silver/gold hoops
- A gold/silver watch
- Pearl earrings (faux or real)
- Shirt dress
- Polo neck top

## CHAPTER 4

A mini masterclass on
*choosing shoes*

*As you will*

probably already know, ladies of 5 ft 3 and under are not all necessarily going to be the Audrey Hepburn's of the world!

However, not surprisingly, some of the most enviable curvaceous and hourglass figures belong to shorter ladies, which is proof that every "body" comes in different shapes and sizes. The most common issue that petite ladies share is finding footwear that neither looks too big for them or too small.

Wearing shoes too small for you can make you appear much larger on the top half of your body, giving you the illusion of incredibly tiny feet and a large upper body even if this is not actually the case. You need to take note of the appearance of a particular pair of shoes around the toe area and note the straps, height and heel too.

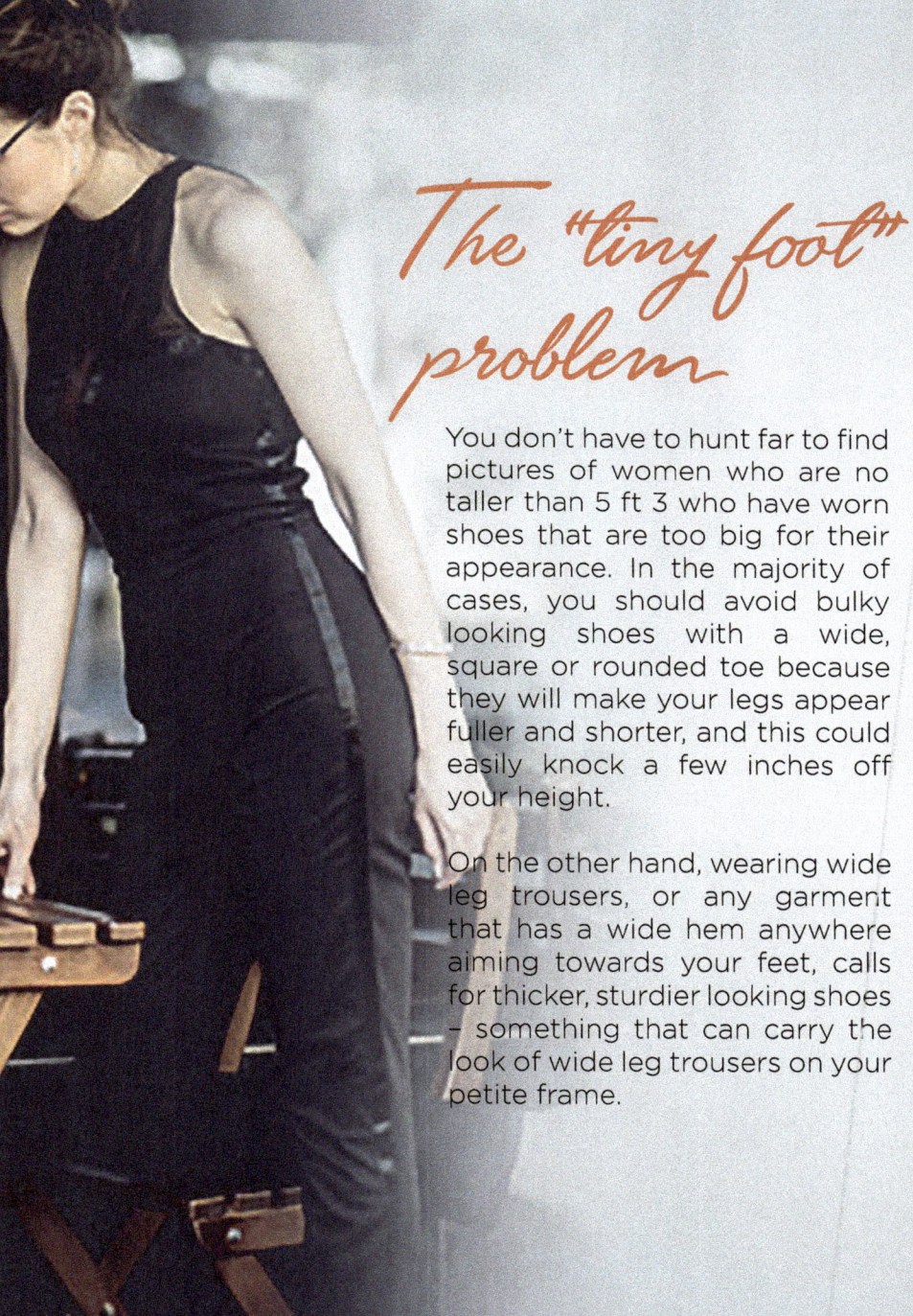

# The "tiny foot" problem

You don't have to hunt far to find pictures of women who are no taller than 5 ft 3 who have worn shoes that are too big for their appearance. In the majority of cases, you should avoid bulky looking shoes with a wide, square or rounded toe because they will make your legs appear fuller and shorter, and this could easily knock a few inches off your height.

On the other hand, wearing wide leg trousers, or any garment that has a wide hem anywhere aiming towards your feet, calls for thicker, sturdier looking shoes – something that can carry the look of wide leg trousers on your petite frame.

**The look you don't want to create...**
**Top tip:** If you are shopping for footwear and are looking for shoes with a narrow toe but don't want them to make your feet look too tiny and your body out of proportion when wearing them, simply try a pair of pointed toe shoes but with a lower heel, as this will instantly make your feet appear bigger but without losing any of the feminine aspects from the look you were going for

> Open shoes that expose the top part of your foot such as ballet pumps will do a lot of justice for your legs and height

# Shoe Rules:

- When wearing bootleg trousers, you should wear wider shoes because pointy heels and narrow shoes will give your body an inverted triangle shape, meaning that your shoulders, bust and waist will seem very broad in comparison with your feet which will appear very small as a result of this poor shoe choice. You should opt for a round or square toe shoe with a thick flat, platform or block heel rather than a stiletto heel.

- When wearing skirts and dresses of any length, other than wearing the look with flip-flops, you should aim to wear daintier shoes, such as pointed toe shoes with smaller, thinner heels. In this case you should avoid ankle straps, thick heels and wide toe shoes.

- Where you can, try to avoid brightly coloured footwear because doing so will shorten and widen the look of your legs and footwear.

- As for boots, try to avoid lengths over the knee or slightly over the ankle. Boots should be ankle boots or knee length but nothing in between or over these specified heights.

- Open shoes that expose the top part of your foot such as ballet pumps will do a lot of justice for your legs and height.

- Ankle straps will "cut off" your legs, making them appear much shorter because that important, delicate 1cm ankle strap is precious room on 29" or below legs. Go for open front shoes in the warmer weather or for formal occasions when possible.

- Ankle boots and shoes with laces at the front will elongate your legs in a balanced way that won't affect the appearance of your legs. On the other hand, zips, tassels and other accessories to the side of shoes and boots (either on the inside of the leg or on the outside of the leg) will add bulk to your legs and could risk you losing definition in your legs.

- In most cases, you should look for boots that are fitted and are not too wide towards the top.

# Top tips

When Choosing Shoes:

- Get sized up properly.
- Invest in a few decent pairs that fit you really well. This will save you heaps of time, effort and money in the long-run.
- Be mindful of the types of outfits you will be wearing with your shoes. Make sure that the shoes till look balanced with the outfit you are wearing – see the tips above for more advice on this!

• SHOES NOT TO WEAR

• SHOES TO WEAR

**CHAPTER 5**

# Dressing for your *skin tone*

If you have ever been shopping and found that some colours just do not suit your colouring and features, then it is because that colour (or more specifically – that shade of colour) does not suit your skin tone.

In order to find out which colours suit your skin tone, you will need to take into account the natural appearance and colour of the following 4 features:

- Your eye colour
- Your (natural) hair colour
- Your natural eyelash and eyebrow colour
- The appearance of your skin – such as a presence of undertones? Do you have freckles?

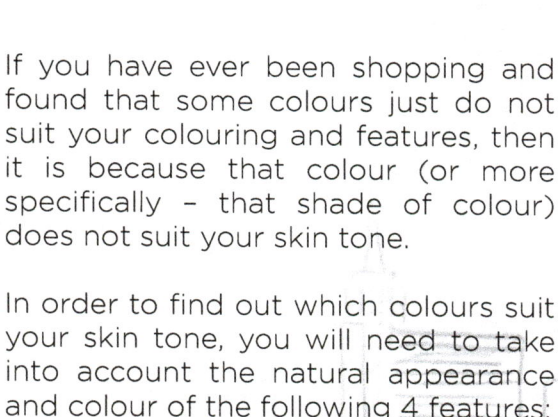

## Determine Your Skin Tone

Determining what kind of skin tone you have can get very complicated, as there are numerous types of skin tones that are incredibly specific to each person.

Determining which of these is your skin tone can get very complicated and is best left to a professional but what you can do is determine whether your skin tone is cool or warm, this of which can easily be done at home and will solve half of your colour-related style issues!are incredibly specific to each person.

**Your skin tone may be:**
- Clear and cool
- Clear and warm
- Cool and clear
- Cool and soft
- Deep and cool
- Deep and warm
- Light and cool
- Light and warm
- Soft and cool
- Soft and warm
- Warm and clear
- Warm and soft

**Cool Skin Tones:**
- A "cool" skin tone means that you have more ash tones in your hair/eyebrow colour than you do red, auburn and warm brown tones.

- Your skin tone is most likely cool if:

- Your veins on your wrist are blue – not green.

- If your eyes are light/blue or green

- Your natural hair, eyebrow and eyelash colour are dark blonde/light brown to medium brown

**Warm Skin Tones:**
- A "warm" skin tone means that
- you have more red/auburn/gold tones in your hair/eyebrow colour than you do ash/non-warm tones.

- Your skin tone is most likely cool if:

- Your veins on your wrist are green – not blue.

- If your eyes are warm/brown/dark blue/green

- Your natural hair, eyebrow and eyelash colour are auburn/light blonde/medium brown to black.

Take the
# *"Pink test"*

Take a bright pink item of clothing and place it next to your face. Does it bring out the pink in your cheeks in a very flattering way or does it make your whole face look red and blotchy?

Ignore how you feel about the colour pink, just observe how it makes your skin tone look. Is it flattering or unflattering? Does it compliment your skin tone or highlight imperfections?

# Cool skin tone

If you have a cool skin tone and/or your skin appears blotchy when doing the above "pink test" then you should stick to cooler colours that balance out any redness in your skin. These colours are often referred to as spring/summer colours because these colour palettes are made up of spring and summer-influenced colours, such as lilac, blue, green, etc.

Here are some examples of colours and tones that would suit you best.

# Warm skin tone

If you have a warm skin tone and/or the above "pink test" shows off your skin tone in a flattering way then you should opt for warmer colours that bring out your rosy cheeks that are often disguised by your warmer, olive-type complexion.

These colours are often referred to as autumn/winter colours because these colour palettes are made up of autumn and winter-influenced colours, such as burgundy, orange, emerald green, etc.

Here are some examples of colours and tones that would suit you best.

**CHAPTER 6**

Using colour to dress for your
*body shape*

**Mixing Colours well**

The reason so many people struggle with matching different colours that go well together is because they are choosing from a much larger colour range, rather than choosing from the colour palette suited to their own personal skin tone. Once you know which colours truly suit you, you can mix and match any of these colours and they will instantly compliment your skin tone & features, and these colours chosen will also complement each other too because they will be from a similar colour palette.

## Creating Colour Confidence

The key to dressing well and feeling great is to wear and buy 80% of styles and colours that suit you and 20% of things that you love too much to care how much they suit you. There will be colours that are supposed to suit your skin tone well but just because they suit your skin tone it doesn't mean that you are guaranteed to like them and that's ok. If you do not like a particular colour, you don't feel confident in it or perhaps it makes you feel depressed then simply don't wear it - you don't have to! Stick to colours that you like but work out the best way to wear them first! You may prefer some colours in the form of an accessory such as a handbag, necklace, scarf, pair of earrings, etc. If you want to become more daring with colour, either take the plunge and wear the colours that you have not yet dared to wear or make the process a gradual one by choosing a smaller item or an accessory in that shade at first so that you get used to seeing that colour on you.

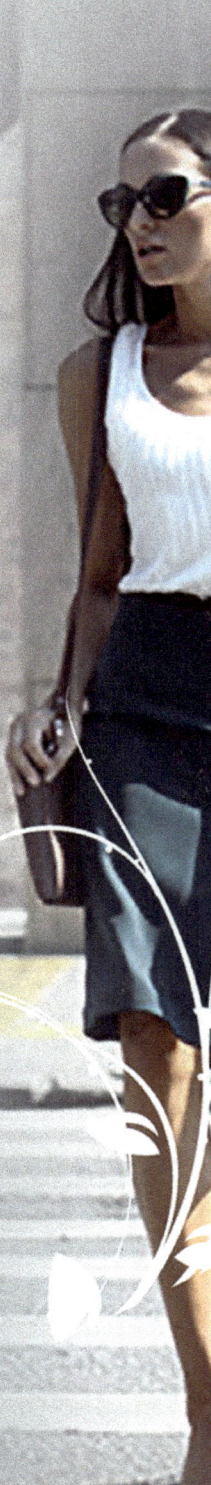

# The Psychcology of *Colour* on our Moods, Feelings and Behaviour

# The Psychology of Colour on our Moods, Feelings and Behaviour

## Cool Colours

Colour is a powerful force in our lives and can have a profound effect on our bodies and minds.

Colours in the blue side of the spectrum are known as cool colours and can invoke feelings ranging from calm to sadness or indifference.

See our chart beside on the possible effects on your mood as well as possible reactions of others depending on the colour you choose to wear.

**Dark Green #2b5846**
Restful, hushed, reliable, prosperity, stately, trustworthy

**Foliage Greens #39754a**
Fertile, healthy, growth, soothing, harmony, restful, restoration

**Bright Green #49a368**
Fresh, grass, Irish, lively, spring, renewal, lush

**Emerald #4aa28c**
Luxurious, jewel-like, up-scale, ritzy, expensive

**Aqua #a0dad3**
Airy, refreshing, cleansing

**Turquoise #7bc7bd**
Infinity, compassion, protective, faithful, tropical

**Teal #337c91**
Serene, cool, tasteful, sophisticated, confident

**Sky Blue #93bdcd**
Heavenly, true, dependable, restful, tranquil, open, reassuring

**Light Blue #afcbe4**
Calm, quiet, patient, tranquility, peace, expansive

**Periwinkle #93a7d3**
Genial, lively, sprightly, convivial, cordial

**Bright Blue #3889c2**
Electric, brisk, vibrant, energy, stirring, impressive, exhilarating

**Deep Blue #343f79**
Credible, authoritative, basic, conservative, strong, reliable

**Lavender #ba66a3**
Romantic, nostalgic, fanciful, lightweight, lightly scented

**Mauve #ab8da0**
Wistful, sentimental, thoughtful, compassionate

**Amethyst #c09ec2**
Curative, protective, peace of mind, calming

**Blue Purple #74519b**
Contemplative, meditative, spiritual, mysterious, enchanting

**Red Purple #8b4f9f**
Sensual, thrilling, witty, intensely exciting, dramatic, expressive

**Deep Purple #4a2d5b**
Visionary, rich, royal, prestigious, subduing, distant, introspective

**Neutral Grey #9c9c9d**
Classic, sober, corporate, timeless, quiet, logical, deliberate

**Charcoal Grey #696c6f**
Steadfast, responsible, staunch, accountable, enduring

**Taupe #b7b29d**
Practical, timeless, authentic, organic, versatile, understated

**Cream**
Soft, subtle, cozy, dusky, gentle, composed, nostalgic

**Silver (Metallic)**
Sleek, classy, sedate, modern, cool, unique

**Black #000000**
Empowered, elegant, mysterious, sophisticated, bold, classic, sober

**White #ffffff**
Pure, clean, pristine, virginal, spotless, innocent, silent, airy

# Warm Colours

## The Psychology of Colour on our Moods, Feelings and Behaviour

Colour is a powerful force in our lives and can have a profound effect on our bodies and minds.

Colours in the red area of the colour spectrum are known as warm colours and can evoke emotions ranging from warmth and comfort to anger and hostility.

See our chart below on the possible effects on your mood as well as possible reactions of others depending on the colour you choose to wear.

**Deep Red #ad4157**
Rich, elegant, refined, tasty, expensive, mature, sumptuous

**Brick Red #7e3b40**
Earthy, warm, strong, sturdy, established, country

**Bright Red #ca4747**
Exciting, energizing, passionate, powerful, dynamic, sexy, assertive

**Bright Pink #c0698d**
Theatrical, playful, high-energy, sensual, wild, tropical, flirty

**Dusty Pink #da4b8e**
Soft, subtle, cozy, dusky, gentle, composed, nostalgic

**Light Pink #f0c0c8**
Sweet, wholesome, soft, understated, innocent, light

**Peach #ffccaa**
(illegible)

**Coral #e99c8d**
Life force, energizing, hostility, desire, comforting

**Tangerine #eda45c**
Vim, juice, truth, energising, tangy, youthful

**Vibrant Orange #e68751**
Fun, whimsical, childlike, happy, active, glowing, friendly, expansive, jovial

**Ginger #c45950**
Spicy, flavorful, tangy, pungent, exotic, hot

**Terra Cotta #bd826f**
Earthy, country, wholesome, welcoming, abundance, warm

**Tan #c0946e**
Rugged, outdoor, rustic, woodsy, grounded

**Chocolate Brown #734d3e**
Delicious, rich, appetizing, robust, mouth watering

**Earth Brown #6a5c56**
Steady, solid, rooted, sheltering, warm, durable, secure, reliable

**Gold (Metallic)**
Bling, rich, divine, intuitive, luxurious, opulent, valuable, radiant

**Amber #439252**
Jewelry, multi-cultural, mellow, abundant, original, autumn

**Golden Yellow #ceb959**
Warming, buttery, tasty, sunny, comfort, palatable

**Bright Yellow #f0d65c**
Joyful, stimulating, gold, moody, energetic, vigour

**Light Yellow #f5e391**
Cheering, happy, soft, sunny, warming, sweet, easy, pleasing

**Chartreuse #cbd853**
Key lime, tasty, alarming, stop, pungent

**Light Green #c3f0a9**
Calm, quiet, restrue, light, natural

**Olive Green #919e67**
Military, camouflage, safari, classic, outdoorsy

**Lime #93a762**
Fresh, citrusy, youthful, acidic, tart, refreshing

**CHAPTER 7**

# Creating curves through
## *clothing*

You have probably noticed in the media how fashion and lifestyle magazines, as well as other forms of media aimed at women are filled with articles on diets and tips for losing weight or appearing slimmer. So what if you want to create curves or appear fuller in figure?! There are more ladies out there in this position than you may think so you are not alone! Of course, you need to know just a few simple rules in order to achieve the illusion of curves in a clever and stylish way rather than looking frumpy and your dress sense misunderstood!

## FASHION STYLING TIP 1:
## A Peplum Hem is Your New Best Friend!

A peplum hem has "built-in" curves, as do ruffles, frills, lace, ruched garments and other textures that create volume and angles to your figure. When it comes to creating curves, you should not wear well-fitted, slim-fitting clothing, as the way to create curves is to mix varying fits and textures to create a well balanced figure. A peplum hem top for example, will give the illusion of an hourglass shaped top half, where the peplum hem at the bottom of a skirt will give the illusion of fuller hips and thighs. Ruffles on a blouse will add bulk to your bust and stomach area and ruching at the sides of tops and on the shoulders gives a more obvious waste and forms an hourglass appearance, whereas the shoulder ruching will give you more defined shoulders.

## FASHION STYLING TIP 2:
## Attention to Detail Best Friend!

Unlike if you wanted to appear slimmer and leaner, you do not have to worry about avoiding any loud prints or tiny detail on clothing when trying to create a fuller figure – the more the better. Big patterns, tiny detail, heavy materials and horizontal stripes are all great patterns to wear in order to look stylish and add about 10lbs instantly and to all of the right places. Note: horizontal stripes work best for adding curves; vertical stripes work best for making you look slimmer. You can also wear combat trousers and other more detailed clothing styles, which would usually add "bulk" and "volume" to many figures, but don't worry – you can afford to!

## FASHION STYLING TIP 3:
## Change Where You Shop Best Friend!

If you are not a teenager do not shop in teenage fashion stores. Teenage fashion clothes are designed for teenage girls and therefore give you a very child-like appearance when wearing these garments. Instead of shopping in the kids section, go to the petite section of adult fashion stores where you will find a range of "shaper" jeans, plus varying styles, fits and cuts. It may sound like hard work, but spending a little extra time looking for the right places that stock petite wear and that can cater for your needs will save you lots of cash and style frustration later on!

**CHAPTER 8**

# Balancing Out
your body proportions

long body and short legs/ short body long legs / big chested (busty), big stomach, big arms, big butt, flat butt.

Every woman in the world has one part of her body that she feels is her "problem area." Catwalk models are considered flawless, but due to their lack of curves they often have flatter bottoms. Ladies with enviable hourglass figures often hate their upper arms...the list goes on. In some cases, no amount of exercise or strict diets will fix these problem areas, but don't worry because the next best thing is dressing to improve, fix or hide these areas!

women are now choosing to wear hipster and low rise trousers and jeans, which is preventing them from developing accentuated waists

## LONG BODY, SHORT LEGS

**Fact:** Longer bodies and shorter legs is a body shape that is now becoming increasingly common in this day and age! Why? Because girls and women are now choosing to wear hipster and low rise trousers and jeans, which is preventing them from developing accentuated waists. Years ago, girls from as young as 13/14 would wear waist enhancing underwear and clothing in order to develop the perfect hourglass figure where their bust and hips would be at least 9 inches wider than their waist measurement. These days not many girls or women under the age of 50 wear high waisted trousers unless they happen to be in fashion, which is why today's women have less of a difference in their waist, bust and hip measurements. This then has a domino effect on the length of their upper bodies, because regular wear of hipster jeans has lead to their bodies establishing a much lower hip line. To sum up, their hip lines will be lower meaning that their upper body will be longer – sometimes appearing almost as long as their legs.

The Fix: The best way to fix this both short-term and long-term is to start wearing higher waistbands. Wearing a waist band that reaches your bellybutton or just below will shorten the appearance of your upper body, whilst making your legs appear longer. Should you adapt this new style habit long-term, you may even be able to permanently retrain your body to establish a higher hipline and create a more obvious waist. Opt for higher waistlines on your skirts, trousers and jeans and wear shorter tops that sit above your hips.

> women are now choosing to wear hipster and low rise trousers and jeans, which is preventing them from developing accentuated waists

## SHORT BODY, LONG LEGS

Fact: Typically, it is apple shaped women who suffer shorter upper bodies and longer legs. The issue that many ladies with shorter upper bodies find is that having a shorter upper body makes them appear fuller on their top half - another common issue for apple shapes. Even in petite ladies, it is possible for you to have an inside leg of 28/29 which is classed as regular in trouser sizes however, your upper body may be much shorter in comparison.

The Fix: You should opt for tailored fitting tops so as not to drown your upper body. When choosing tops and jackets choose slim fitting styles that come down to your hip bone, as this will elongate the look of your upper body. In terms of sleeves, choose long sleeved tops or t-shirts with standard short sleeves – strap and sleeveless varieties are best avoided when trying to elongate the look of your upper body.

Is you bust more than 10 inches larger than your waistline or is there less than a 10 inch difference?

# Big Chest / Big Bust

> Avoid short tops and jackets that sit above your hip bone.

Fact: When trying to disguise or dress down a larger bust, you need to be perfectly clear on whether your bust is more than 10 inches larger than your waistline or is there less than a 10 inch difference? If there is less than a 10 inch difference then you're more likely to be apple shaped and should consult the advice below on dressing down a larger waistline and upper body. If your bust is 10 or more inches bigger than your waistline then your bust indeed will be one of your fullest measurements, in which case you need to read on.

As you have probably found out, having a fuller bust has as many advantages as it does disadvantages. Although many of your friends may envy your curves, dressing for day to day life can prove challenging. In the right dress or outfit, accentuating a larger bust can appear very sophisticated and feminine however, in your daily life you may want to make your bust appear a little less obvious or simply make it appear in proportion with the rest of your body. In some cases, a fuller bust can make you look up to a couple of sizes larger than you actually are as well, which is why it is useful to know how to balance out your fuller bust.

See below for example

**The Fix:** It can seem tempting and appropriate to wear a baggy top or tunic to completely disguise your bust. This may help you to feel more elegant and slimmer. Unfortunately this is the wrong thing to do! Not only does wearing a baggy, oversized top or tunic make your bust appear the same size or fuller, it also makes the rest of your body covered by the top appear the same size as your widest measurement – which is most likely going to be your bust. You may be surprised to learn that the best way to disguise or reduce a larger bust is to wear fitting upper body garments that come down to your hip bone and also – take note of the neckline which is very important! A narrow neckline will make your bust appear fuller, which is why you should avoid round necks. V-necks are good if you want to accentuate an hourglass figure, but if you want to balance out a fuller chest, opt for wider neck lines, such as:

- Square necks
- Wide round necks
- Wide v-neck tops

*Avoid tops that are very baggy around your waist area*

# WIDER WAISTLINE

Fact: Wider waistlines usually belong to those who have very slim hips. Quite often ladies who have very petite bone structure with narrow shoulders and hips often have wider waistlines. Don't be confused by this although ladies in this category are prone to carrying extra weight around their waistlines, this doesn't always have to be the case, you may just have a less accentuated waist that's not many inches smaller than your hips. Either way, the same rules on dressing a wider waistline will apply.

Avoid short tops and jackets that sit above your hip bone.

## To Fix:

- Stop wearing clothing that doesn't do you any favours. One of the most common habits of all people with less accentuated waistlines is that they choose to wear garments that were made for ladies with different body shapes to theirs.
- You need to choose longer tops and upper body garments which must come down to your hip bone (no higher).
- Avoid short tops and jackets that sit above your hip bone.
- Avoid wearing patterned tops and jackets. Instead stick to plainer colours or if you like wearing patterns, wear patterns on your bottom half and plainer colours on your top half.

- As you do not have a narrow waistline, do not wear clingy belts that sit on your waist. If you have a tiny waist line then these look great but if not, they will only add fullness to your waistline which is not what you want.
- Wear v-neck tops.
- Avoid tops that are very baggy around your waist area.
- If you have slimmer shoulders and arms, choose tops and jackets with well fitting arms and with more detail around the shoulder area, this will give the illusion of (only slightly) slightly fuller shoulders and a narrower waistline.

## WIDER UPPER ARMS

Fact: Your wider upper arms may be down to you carrying more weight on your upper body or down to the fact that you workout a lot both of which can result in wider upper arms.

**The Fix:** You can fix this issue easily through jewellery or sleeves!

- Bigger watches and bracelets will make the tops of your arms appear smaller.
- Wear longer sleeves.
- When wearing t-shirts, find longer sleeves that are slightly longer than standard t-shirt sleeves but not as long as sleeves.
- When wearing longer sleeves, try to find tops that have buttons at the wrists or that are turned up at the wrist or that have some other detail at the wrist. This will take the emphasis off of your upper arms and help to slim and **elongate them.**
- Avoid strap tops.
- Avoid tube tops.
- Avoid sleeveless tops.

When layering your tops, try to wear the same colour but different shades, rather than two or more different colours completely, which will create an extreme contrast and could make your arms appear shorter and wider.

- Avoid strap tops.
- Avoid tube tops.
- Avoid sleeveless tops.
- When layering your tops, try to wear the same colour but different sha es, rather than two or more different colours completely, which will create an extreme contrast and could make your arms appear shorter and wider.

*A Bra can make you look slimmer, curvier, taller, shorter, so getting it paramount to your fashion success*

## WIDER BOTTOM

Fact: Some trousers and bottoms will make your bottom appear wider – even if you do not actually have a wide bottom. Wider bottoms usually mean that your body shape type is pear shape. This means that you have slim arms, a slim top half, small waist but fuller hips, butt and thighs. The mistake than many ladies who fall into this category make is that they create too much of a contrast between their upper and lower body, thus making their upper body appear very narrow and their lower body appear very wide. This is usually because they mix up the patterns and styles that they should actually be wearing in the opposite places, i.e. certain prints are best for their upper bodies, other styles are best for their lower bodies.

The Fix: Combat trousers are many women's "go to" style staple when they have larger thighs, hips and bottoms but this is one of the biggest mistakes you can make and will only make your thighs and butt appear wider even though combats may seem like a sensible option. The buttons and detail on the outer sides of most combat trousers draw attention to these areas and make your lower body appear fuller. Many ladies in this category hate jeans because they fear that jeans will highlight their fuller lower body when in fact, some jeans can actually be a savior!

- Avoid patterned trousers, stick to plainer colours and styles
- Avoid lots of detail on bottoms – i.e. lots of buttons, pockets, zips, etc.
- Keep your bottoms plain and opt for more interesting patterns on top to balance out the difference between your upper and lower body.
- When choosing jeans opt for darker colours or with lighter jeans such as stonewash and white choose a size up or a looser fitting style.
- When choosing jeans, try to find a pair that are dark on the outside of the leg and lighter in the middle. This is like "contouring for legs" – it will shrink the width of your bottom and legs.

- Be mindful when choosing back pockets on trousers.

- If you want to slim down your derrière then opt for larger back pockets and these will make this area look smaller. On the other hand, if you are trying to fake a larger bottom then go for smaller back pockets.

- Avoid thick materials or boxy materials. Choose softer, more moveable fabrics to help prevent further contrast in your body shape.

- Avoid sleeveless tops.

- When layering your tops, try to wear the same colour but different shades, rather than two or more different colours completely, which will create an extreme contrast and could make your arms appear shorter and wider.

## FLAT BOTTOM

Fact: Besides from hourglass figures, every type of body shape can have a flat bottom even of you have fuller legs and wider hips. Although having a flat bottom can be frustrating at times when you try on trousers and jeans in stores and find that you're unable to fill them out like you wanted to, having a smaller bottom means that you can always "add to it." With the help of a little pattern, some well places pockets, stripes, buttons and detail you can easily fake a rounder, pert, and fuller bottom without having to do a single squat!

The Fix: Basically, you need to do everything and wear everything that somebody from the pear shape category shouldn't!

- Back pockets that are close together give the illusion of a toned curved bottom, whereas pockets that are spaced apart will give the illusion of a fuller bottom.

- Wear bottoms with detail around the upper thigh and bottom area.

- Try to choose bottoms with a thick waist band instead of a small, standard waistband. The thicker waistband will accentuate a bottom of any size.

Bigger watches and bracelets will make the tops of your arms appear smaller.
- Wear longer sleeves.
- When wearing t-shirts, find longer sleeves that are slightly longer than standard t-shirt sleeves but not as long as sleeves.
- When wearing longer sleeves, try to find tops that have buttons at the wrists or that are turned up at the wrist or that have some other detail at the wrist. This will take the emphasis off of your upper arms and help to slim and elongate them.
- Avoid strap tops.
- Avoid tube tops.
- Avoid sleeveless tops.

When layering your tops, try to wear the same colour but different shades, rather than two or more different colours completely, which will create an extreme contrast and could make your arms appear shorter and wider.

**CHAPTER 9**

# Bra fitttings

(cups and sizes for petites)
shapewear, underwear, swim suits

Underwear is a loved or loathed kind of topic. Underwear can play such an important role in the way our outfits can appear. One of the most important items of underwear is bras. Bras can change your shape, your appearance, they can make you look slimmer, curvier, taller, shorter... so getting to grips with understanding which bras are for you is very important. Unless you love buying underwear, buying a bra is perhaps a chore to you or something you know you have to do but not something you want to spend too long over when choosing.

Even if you don't want to spend lots of time browsing over which bra to buy, you should go into a store equipped with the basics so that you will instantly know and understand which bra is best for you. There are so many different types of bras to choose from these days so it is only understandable that it can get rather confusing but this is why you need to know the effect that each bra has on your body and appearance. Depending on whether or not you have had children, whether you have a bigger cup size or a wider under bust measurement, the right bra for you will be different to the bras that others may wear.

> If you are petite and have a small frame then wearing a band size that is too large and has straps that are very thick may overpower your delicate frame and narrow shoulders

Have you ever wondered why some bras that were made especially for your (small/normal/large) bust do not look as good as they should? That's because you have to consider the shape of your bust as well as the size.

Generally, there are 4 different types of bras for 4 different bust shapes and sizes.

These are:
- Small bust size
- Normal bust size
- Large bust size
- Lack of breast substance

The latter – lack of breast substance is where many women go wrong when buying bras. Even if you have a large bust, if you lack substance in the upper front part of your breast then some bras for big-busted ladies will not look as flattering as they could.

## So what is breast substance?

Breast substance is the tissue in the top part of your breast; it is the part below your collar bone and is where the breast starts – it is also the "cleavage" part that may sometimes be shown when wearing a low cut top. Instead of choosing large open cups, choose bras with a thick band a lot of support underneath the cups which will help make the top half of your bust appear fuller and more shapely.

Another important point to remember when choosing underwear is the importance of getting measured properly. If you are petite and have a small frame then wearing a band size that is too large and has straps that are very thick may overpower your delicate frame and narrow shoulders.

### Bras for Fuller Busts.

So, if you have a larger, fuller bust you will need a lot of support but nothing too bulky as that will drown your frame.

- So, if you have a larger, fuller bust you will need a lot of support but nothing too bulky as that will drown your frame.

- Choose bras with a thick bar a lot of support undernea the cups which will he make the top half of yo bust appear fuller and mo shapely.

### HERE ARE SOME OPTIONS FOR FULLER BUSTS

### BRAS FOR SMALLER BUSTS

## BRAS FOR BUSTS WITH LESS BREAST SUBSTANCE

If you are petite and have a small frame then wearing a band size that is too large and has straps that are very thick may overpower your delicate frame and narrow shoulders.

# Shapewear

Let's not also forget the use of shapewear! Shapewear has become increasingly popular over recent years due to the fact that it is affordable and can easily reduce the look of your body weight and shrink your shape by inches and pounds in an instant! Shapewear is a type of underwear that can be worn under your normal garments. Shapewear "pulls you in" like how an old fashioned corset would do but minus the pain, complicated application and discomfort. There are various types of shapewear available, some include:

- Shapewear for legging
- Shapewear for your bu
- Shapewear for your stomach
- Upper body shapewea - tightening the appearance of all of yc upper body
- Lower body shapewea - tightening the appearance of all of yc lower body r wider/ful

*Mastering the perfect underwear is great, but what about swimwear? Usually, whenever you come to wear swimwear you are most likely to be in public, which is why you want to look your best. In order to look your best in swimwear (no matter your size or age), you need to find the right kind of swimwear for your shape.*

*If you have a small bust or lack substance in the upper part of your breasts then here are some excellent suggestions on the right kind of (flattering) swimwear for you. As you will see, some of these show more detail around the chest and neck area, which will add the illusion of fullness to your upper body and bust area, giving you a more balanced figure.*

If you have a larger or fuller bust then these swimsuits and bikinis would be better for you, as they will suit your body shape more, emphasizing your curves but without looking distasteful or too revealing.

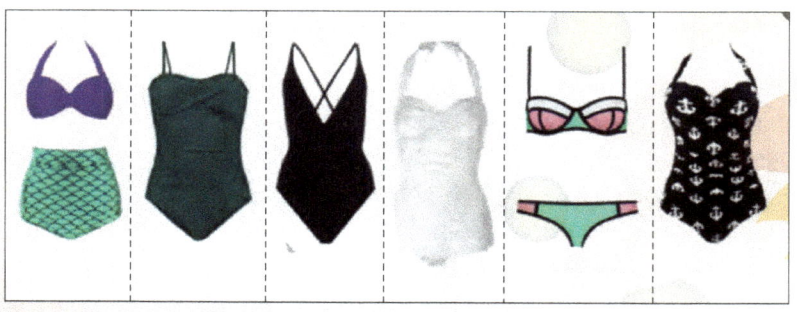

**CHAPTER 10**

# Using jewellery

to balance your body proportions

## TOP TIPS:

- Large bracelets and watches slim down and elongate your fingers, wrists, hands, forearms, upper arms and waist area.
- Small bracelets and watches add fullness to your fingers, wrists, hands, forearms, upper arms and waist area.
- Small rings slim down and elongate your fingers, wrists, hands, forearms, upper arms and waist area.
- Large rings add fullness to your fingers, wrists, hands, forearms, upper arms and waist area.
- Long earrings, single-colour earrings, earrings that sit against your face slim down your face, chin and neck.

Wide, rounder, small, detailed, colourful earrings make your face, chin and neck appear fuller, shorter and rounder.

Thick chain/decorative, costume jewellery-type short length necklaces shorten your neck but make the top half of your body appear smaller.

Thin, long chains elongate your neck but neither slim or increase the size of your body.

Thin, short chains shorten the length of your neck and make your upper body appear wider/fuller.

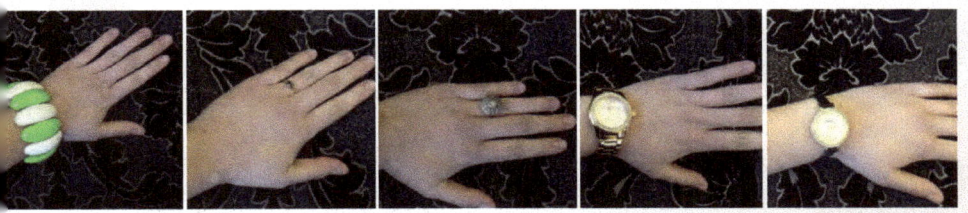

**CHAPTER 11**

Using other *accessories* to dress

There are so many items that you need to consider when getting dressed for the day. As well as finding the right clothing to fit your shape, you also need to find the right accessories that will suit you as well.

During the year, other items such as hats, scarves, glasses and handbags prove as very important for practical reasons and to polish off a desired look.

Finding accessories to suit your size and height is actually one of the most enjoyable and easiest parts of dressing.

As a petite lady because you can go into almost any store and find something that will suit you perfectly. Quite often, ladies who fall into the category of petite tend to go wild buying accessories on a shopping trip but are more likely to be unsuccessful when buying clothing or footwear! (That is until Petitepeds arrived!! www.petitepeds.com.au )

However there are few things that can go wrong when shopping for accessories. But with a few points to consider to steer you in the right direction, accessory shopping will be a breeze!

# Hats

Don't be afraid of hats! Hats are extremely practical in the very hot and very cool weather. Having a bad hair day? It's hats to the rescue! In a rush and don't have time to do your hair? Throw on a hat and instantly look cool and stylish in seconds – nobody will ever know that you're hiding messy hair underneath! The right hat can add height to your frame, whereas the wrong hat can make you appear shorter. Some hats can look extremely flattering, whereas others can drown a narrow frame.

Don't be afraid of hats! Hats are extremely practical in the very hot and very cool weather. Having a bad hair day? It's hats to the rescue! In a rush and don't have time to do your hair? Throw on a hat and instantly look cool and stylish in seconds – nobody will ever know that you're hiding messy hair underneath! The right hat can add height to your frame, whereas the wrong hat can make you appear shorter. Some hats can look extremely flattering, whereas others can drown a narrow frame.

When choosing hats you want to avoid:

- Huge, oversized hats.
- Hats with bows on them.
- Hats with ribbons that hang in front of your face.
- Cowboy style hats with an under the chin tie

Hats to consider include:

- Round hats that are not too wide
- Baseball caps
- Small hats
- Bobble hats with a bobble on top (the bobble will add height to your body)
- Trilby hats

# Scarves

Scarves are an accessory that can keep you warm in the winter, as well as make an outfit look smarter or more casual in the right situation. You will see that there are often various styles of scarves available, from those that are very short and used as wrist scarves, silk scarves used for fashion purposes, shawls, snoods and thick winter scarves. Different types of scarves suit di ferent people. For e.g. short scarves rarely suit tall people, whereas long, oversized scarves look too overpowering for anybody who is apple shaped or under 5 ft 5. You will see many fashion models wearing very long, oversized scarves which may be up to 2 metres long in length and 30cm wide, but these can be very difficult to wear if you are not 5 ft 9 with a straight type of body shape. Wearing a scarf that is too long will cover the majority of your body, on the other hand tying it and folding it will add bulk around your neck and chest area, which will again make you look several inches shorter, as well as out of proportion.

## Scarf Definitions:

- Thick winter scarf: long scarves worn in the winter, varying in length (some are short and others are very long and can span the entire length of your body).
- Snood: a round scarf that sits comfortably around your neck. These can come in woollen varieties or softer, lighter varieties and depending on the material used they can be worn all year round. Snoods do not have two end pieces like a typical scarf, they are round and can be simply put round your neck and doubled up if too long – they make putting on a scarf quick and easy.
- Shawl: shawls (see below) are used as a cover up on the beach and can also be worn with formal wear, such as with a dress. Shawls are an excellent alternative to light jackets and cardigans..

Here are some scarves that will suit you perfectly. Note how they are not as long, but how it is still quite possible to find an excellent range of stylish and attractive scarves for all purposes and seasons.

- Scarves with pointed ends such as the first picture below will give the illusion of a slimmer, taller figure.
- Also, experiment with different ways of tying your scarf, as some people find it more comfortable to wear their scarf in certain styles which perhaps suit them better.

# Glasses

The type of glasses and sunglasses that will suit you will depend on your face shape and personal preferences. The most important point to remember when choosing glasses is not the style and shape but the width of the glasses. The most common problem that affects petite ladies more than anybody else when shopping for glasses is that they often end up buying "on-trend" styles which are actually too big for their smaller bone structure. This issue affects petite ladies of all weights and body shape, no matter your face shape or any other contributing factor. Many curvier ladies at 5 ft 2 who have round face shapes suffer this problem too because they buy and wear sunglasses that are too wide for their face and forehead. To avoid this problem, make sure that when testing out glasses (sunglasses or normal glasses) that the sunglasses do not come away from your face – they should not exceed the width of your head.

- The best shape sunglasses for petite ladies are those with smaller frames. Wayfarer sunglasses and smaller aviator sunglasses are an excellent option, as well as round sunglasses and cat eye sunglasses with smaller frames and lenses. Here below are some excellent options for you that won't overpower or hide all of your face.
- Top tip: If you have stronger, more defined bone structure then choose softer frames. If you have less defined bone structure then choose thicker, heavier frames.

> The best shape sunglasses for petite ladies are those with smaller frames.

# Handbags

The good news about finding handbags that will compliment your height and shape is that you can wear any size handbag and it will look great!

The bad news is that you need to pay attention to the shape!

Wide, oversized handbags that appear "floppy" and untailored are not ideal for ladies under 5ft3. Wide handbags in general are best avoided because they can easily add fullness to the point of your body at which they sit, such as under your shoulder, at your waist, at your hips or near your thighs. Large, oversized handbags that resemble the style of beach bags can also make you appear far shorter than you really are, because these kinds of bags can actually make you look as though you are carrying luggage rather than a handbag.

# Handbags

What you want to look for are bags that are longer in length rather than wide and try to choose bags that look more tailored in design, rather than bags that have no obvious shape.

Longer straps are an excellent idea too, as these will elongate your upper body and legs. Remember that you can wear both small and large bags, just make sure that when choosing larger handbags that you choose handbags that are longer, more tailored in appearance and that have a prominent shape to them.

Here are some fantastic styles to choose from:

## CHAPTER 12

### How to dress to suit your *age*

There are so many advantages to being a petite woman, such as:

- You can alter your height as and when you like, enjoying the option of being shorter or taller with the help of heels.

- You can enjoy getting yourself a bargain when shopping in the sales, because you're not the "standard" height.

- You will always look very feminine.

- You suit almost any item of clothing (provided that it's the right fit and style).

- And, you can enjoy looking younger for longer.

There are so many advantages to being a petite woman, such as:

- You can alter your height as and when you like, enjoying the option of being shorter or taller with the help of heels.

- You can enjoy getting yourself a bargain when shopping in the sales, because you're not the "standard" height.

- You will always look very feminine.

- You suit almost any item of clothing (provided that it's the right fit and style).

- And, you can enjoy looking younger for longer.

The latter doubles up as one of the pros and cons of being slightly shorter in height. Whilst it is great to remain looking youthful for longer, there are of course cases when you do not want to look like a teenager! One of the main misconceptions about dressing for your age and dressing to look more sophisticated is that you have to wear heels – this is not always the case.

The key to dressing to look older and more sophisticated so that you do not get mistaken for a child is to dress in a simple but more sophisticated way.

So what does this mean?
There are certain styles and patterns that are often considered as "younger/teen" types of prints. You should avoid making these mistakes and wearing any of these items if you want to appear older when you dress. Here is what you should avoid:

Loud prints
Bold slogans
Skinny jeans
Leggings
Baggy clothing
Anything with a hood
Jeans or leggings tucked into knee length boots
Bright colours
Neon colours
Trainers
Bomber jackets

Here is a list of items that are perfect if you want to look older and smarter when dressing, or if you simply don't want to be mistaken for a teenager:

- Straight leg or bootleg jeans
- Ankle boots
- A tailored style handbag
- Cardigans with delicate button detail
- Pointed toe shoes
- Rich, more expensive looking colours, such as burgundy, light grey, cream, black and white.
- Trench coats
- Blazers
- Plainer clothing with little to no pattern
- A gold or silver watch
- A cross-body bag (worn as a clutch or on one shoulder)
- Shirts and blouses
- Pencil skirts

What is Style and how to

*achieve it?*

**CHAPTER 13**

Style is not about being fashionable or dressed to perfection 365 days a year, it is about being stylish, comfortable and confident 365 days a year.

Style is a way in which one wears something and presents themselves. Usually a unique way or at least a way that is most comfortable for that person.

Don't confuse style with fashion! It is the biggest mistake that so many people make and this, along with other factors causes confusion. Fashion is the "this and now", it is trends that are popular now. Style however is different. Style is infinitive. We know that we need to develop and understand our own style before we start to develop a wardrobe that we are happy with, but how do we go about doing so? You must start with the basics and not get wrapped up in current fashion trends, designer brands and fashion magazines showcasing how you should dress.

The reason why so many people go wrong with dressing well is because they try to run before they can walk. They go from wearing their tracksuits and comfies one day to wearing an overly detailed outfit possibly fit for a wedding or other special occasion the next day. The result? It never lasts. They revert back to their old ways and why not?!

Because that high maintenance style that they thought was right is simply not for them. You'll know that you have found your true style when it feels comfortable and not hard work. Don't get me wrong – you can still look fabulous and glamorous but you have to do it your own way and that is what's so special about personal style building.

Here's a little secret that few people have yet to realise or care to admit: each emerging fashion trend is not a matter of one-size-fits-all. It would be impossible for anybody who is not a catwalk model to carry off each and every fashion look. Following fashion trends religiously without developing your own personal style where you know what suits you is the same as only ever using a sat nav when driving – you can get to places and maybe the sat nav route is not the best, most convenient or the quickest but without your trusty sat nav you would be lost!

> we need to develop and understand our own style before we start to develop a wardrobe that we are happy with

Having your own

*personal style*

gives you the confidence to accept those off-days and makes you feel comfortable within yourself. Having your own personal style is like having your own brand, you know what it's about, what is not relevant and what would/wouldn't suit it. When you develop your own personal style, you will find shopping so much easier, more enjoyable and far quicker than when you don't know where to start.

As mentioned before, your wardrobe should be made up of 80% clothes and accessories that really suit you and 20% of items that you love too much to care whether they don't suit as well as others. This is the key to a happy wardrobe and creating your own unique style.

Here are some fabulous tips to help you develop and maintain your own super style:

- How tall are you? What is your natural skin tone? What size are you now? Don't think about the skin colour you may have after your two week holiday abroad later in the year, don't think about what will suit you when you are a few lbs lighter or heavier, and don't think about your height when wearing your heels. The way to build great style is being honest with yourself and taking yourself as you are today – pale skin, love handles and all!

- If you love wearing certain clothes but they don't flatter your body shape or skin tone then customise them slightly so that they do suit you, i.e. if you love stripes but you want to avoid horizontal stripes because they make you appear wider, opt for vertical stripes which will elongate and slim out your body.

- If and when you do not feel 100% confident with your weight or appearance, wear stunning accessories and great footwear instead. This will make you feel amazing, confident and glamorous without drawing attention to your so-called problem areas and will stop you from thinking too much about them!

- Avoid high-end and designer clothing when you are just starting to establish your style brand. Designer brands are wonderful but they tend to confuse a lot of people who believe (just like when following fashion trends) that they will be instantly stylish if they stick to designers – which is not true. Another issue with designer clothing and accessories is that you may be so keen to wear them constantly that you never feel stylish or adequate when you are not decked out in brand names.

- Keep it simple! Tackle and master one aspect of your style day by day. Don't copy somebody else's look, especially not a drastic look. Don't rush into buying cloting, footwear or accessories that are overly expensive if you are not completely sure they fit well with your style brand!

Creating your own style and discovering what looks good and suits you may sound like a mammoth task, so you need to take it one step at a time:

1. Start by mastering your perfect look. What do you wear most often? If it's jeans a t-shirt then work on finding the best type of jeans for you (and in the right shades and colours) and look out for the best tops, shirts and jackets that look best too. Perfecting your most worn and most favourite look first will make you feel more confident instantly and will give you the motivation to master other looks too.
2. Go through each look that you would typically wear or would like to wear and experiment with each to find a way of wearing each look to suit your body shape, height, skin tone and of course, your own style tastes! As mentioned above, start with your most favourite and most worn style first before moving on to others. Move through perfecting your best/ideal casual wear look, your best look for the gym, your best formal look, your best summer look, the best coat, the best way to wear bright colours, the best way to wear black, the best way to wear nudes.
3. Remember, a few well fitting garments that you are actually going to wear is much better than a wardrobe full of clothes that you are never going to wear!

TOP TIP: open your wardrobe and ask yourself: how does it make you feel? Do you love the majority of clothes in your wardrobe? Do you love them but don't know how to put them together? Learning these all important style basics, such as how to dress for your body shape, height and skin tone will provide you with the knowledge needed in order not to make mistakes when shopping for clothes or when putting outfits together.

TOP TIP: If the idea of changing the way you transform your clothing into outfits scares you then it is a good idea to spare a little time each week to plan your outfits for the following week. Put aside just 20 minutes each Sunday for example, to put together complete outfits which you can then fold up or hang up in your wardrobe so that you can simply pull them out again as and when you need them, thereby making your morning routine much quicker and far less stressful!

## CHAPTER 14

What Not to *Wear...*

# Underwear...

In some cases, some outfits and styles can be worn by one person well but may not suit another person at all, in which case we would say that the second person should not wear that item or look. For e.g. a tall lady of 5 ft 9 could get away with wearing shoes with a thick ankle strap, whereas a lady of 5 ft 1 should avoid shoes with thick ankle straps because they would significantly "shorten" her legs. On the other hand, there are certain dressing and style rules that apply to everyone because there are a definite "no, no!"

- Be mindful of what you plan to wear when choosing your bra. Under no circumstances does a black bra or a coloured bra look good under a pale shirt. When choosing underwear, it is safest to stick to these three colours: nude/skin colour, black and white.

- Do you wear bras that are too big for you? You must ensure that you wear the right bra and cup size because under a fitted top, it will be visible if your cup size is too big because the bra cup will be very clear to see.

- Do you wear bras that are too tight or too small? The issue with this is that you will get back "overspill" which means your skin and/or curves will hand over the straps of your bra. This is very visible through t-shirts also and just like in any case when you are "spilling out" of your clothing, it is very unflattering too!

- Make sure that your chosen underwear does not exceed the rise of your trousers/bottoms. Your trousers/skirt should not be lower than the rise of your underwear.

WHAT NOT TO WEAR:
The Ultimate Style Rules and Guide to Good Dressing

# Etiquette

- In some cases such as in your working environment, you may not be allowed to wear low cut tops which expose too much of your cleavage or your skin in general.

  In this case you will need to either wear something else or cover up your cleavage and bare skin.

  You can do this by wearing a crop top under your shirt, wearing a vest top underneath, or using a brooch to pin the shirt together at a slightly higher point so that it's not as low cut or revealing.

# Sizing Mistakes

- "Your clothes should be tight enough to show you're a woman but loose enough to show you're a lady" – Marilyn Monroe. This is one of the most correct statements about style and fit. It doesn't manner how slim or toned you are, extremely tight fitting clothing is not flattering. Extremely tight clothing doesn't look very good on anybody. Your clothing should "skim" your body rather than showing every bump, muscle, roll and wrinkle!

> "Your clothes should be tight enough to show you're a woman but loose enough to show you're a lady" – Marilyn Monroe.

- To elaborate on the above point, you should not try to squeeze yourself into a size that looks too small on you! Even if you have worn size X all of your life and then go into a store and find that size X is too small and you may need a size or two bigger, do not try to squeeze into your usual size X just because that is the size you wear normally. It doesn't matter how small the size is that you're wearing, if it looks bad and too tight then it's not going to look good at all. Wear the size that looks the best on you, even if that is a size or two bigger than you normally wear. Remember – others around you don't see the size on your labels, they only see how you look in that particular garment/outfit!

- One of the most unflattering ways of dressing is wearing clothing that does not fit properly, no matter whether it is too tight or too big. If you want to go for a look that involves wearing oversized clothing then choose clothing that is in your size but has been made to look oversized is the best idea. Unless you are tall and can carry off wearing clothing that's a couple of sizes too big, as a petite woman you can still carry off the look but it is best to stick to oversized versions of sizes that suit your petite frame. Look for "oversized" or "boyfriend" styles stated on clothing labels in stores.

- On the other hand, wearing clothing that is too small and that you "spill out of" is perhaps worse than wearing clothing that is too big. If you struggle to move in your clothing or have to go to great lengths to make them look as though they fit and are not too tight then you probably need a size bigger. Having to leave a button undone or having to spend more than 2 minutes getting a pair of trousers on is a telltale sign that they are perhaps too tight!

- Both of the above style errors devalue the look of an outfit, making it appear far less expensive than what it actually cost. Clothing that is too big or small resembles that of hand-me-downs, something that younger siblings have to experience. Among children it is cute to see them wearing their older sibling's former clothing but in adults it's not a good look. Even if you are on a budget when shopping, it is still possible to find clothing that fits well by observing your natural body shape and sticking only to ga ments and fits that suit your shape!

Top tip for determining whether your clothing is too tight: after you have worn your clothing for a few hours, observe how your body looks afterwards. Are there any marks? Is your skin a different colour in parts (not due to a sun tan but caused by poor fitting clothing)? Not only is wearing extremely tight clothing a bad look in terms of style, you can also risk damaging your health by doing so, as it can restrict blood flow and circulation.

**CHAPTER 15**

A Look-book of Ideal
Clothing And Accessories for

*Petite Ladies*

Handbags

Scarves

Sun glasses

Sun glasses

Scarves

Evening Wear

Evening Wear

Undergarments

Swimsuits

Casual Wear

After 5

Work Wear

Casual Wear

Casual Wear

Dresses & Skirts

**CHAPTER 16**

*Shapes*

# Apple I Pear I Hourglass And Banana/Straight

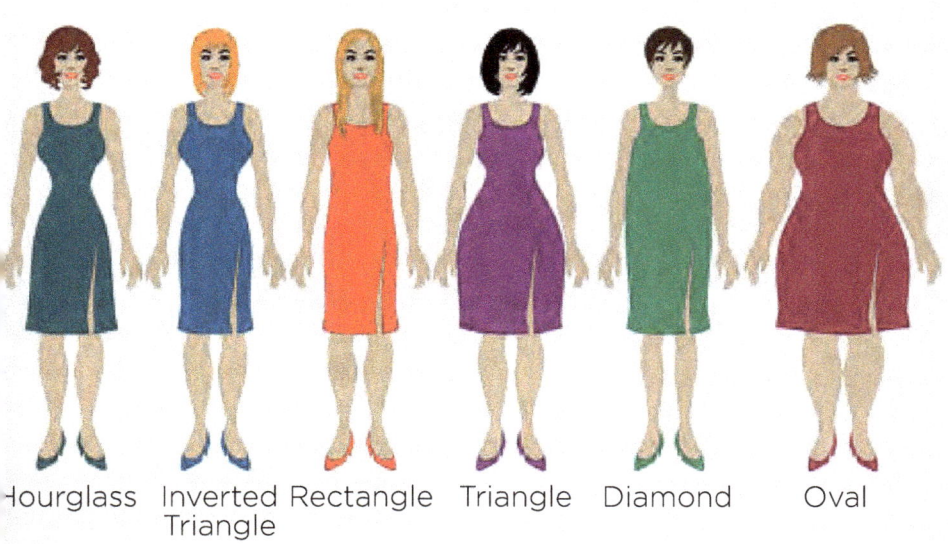

Hourglass | Inverted Triangle | Rectangle | Triangle | Diamond | Oval

# Apple shapes

## What is an Apple Shape?

An apple body shape, as you can see above, is a body shape where the tops of your arms, your bust, waist and sometimes face are rounder or wider than the bottom half of your body. Typically, those with an apple body shape have noticeably thinner legs and a wider upper body. An apple shape body resembles the shape of an inverted triangle – see below.

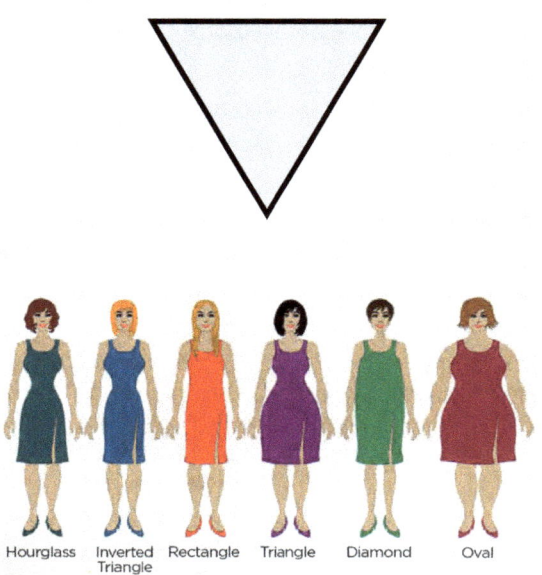

Hourglass    Inverted Triangle    Rectangle    Triangle    Diamond    Oval

The widest point of an apple body shape is around the shoulder or bust area and gradually narrows towards the hips, which are quite often very narrow in comparison. The name "apple shape" represents the rounder appearance of the upper body.

## An Apple Body Shape means:

- Your widest parts of your upper arms, bust, shoulders, waist and possibly, your face or chin area.
- Your hips are very narrow.
- You have slim, lean legs.
- You rarely gain weight on your hips or below.
- You are least one dress size smaller on your bottom half than you are on your top half.

## Adding Height through Clothing

- As somebody with an apple body shape, you will most likely want to add length to your torso. Long, straight fitting tops and jackets are the way to go.

## Adding Height through Clothing

- When choosing jackets, you should never go for anything that sits above your hipbone, and especially not at your waistline.

- Blazers are an excellent option for apple body shapes, provided that you choose styles that sit just above, on or slightly below your hipbone. Also, long lapels on the front of the jacket are a must for slimming down a fuller bust and/or stomach area.

- Many ladies who are apple shapes have fuller upper arms too, in which case you need to avoid strappy tops and tube tops/boob tubes and stick to slim fitting short sleeves and slim fitting long sleeves in the summer. Any detail on the sleeve, such as turn ups, will make your arms appear fuller, which is why it is best to stick to simple styles.

## Elongating Legs & Torso

- Apple shapes usually find that they have shorter bodies, a high hip bone and longer legs. Some ladies who fall into this category of body shape can have an inside leg measurement of 28/29 inches, but the length of their upper body is far shorter. Shorter upper bodies can be difficult to dress because adding even the slightest bit of too much detail can overpower such a small space.

- Skinny trousers and straight leg trousers will elongate your legs. Skinny jeans work better if your upper body is not more than 2 dress sizes larger than your bottom half. Skinny jeans can emphasise the contrast in size and shape between the two halves of your body, which is why slim fitting straight leg jeans that do not grip your ankles at the bottom are the wiser choice.

- When it comes to picking tops, pick loose material that is not too stiff. Fluffy materials or thick woollen jumpers are not a good choice either, as these will make the top half of your body appear fuller. Instead, master the art of layering your clothes gradually.

- A peplum hem on a top will give the illusion of wider hips which will also make your upper body and waist area appear narrower, and is an easy way to fake an hourglass figure.

- In dresses, sleeveless varieties can sometimes work well, provided that the dress comes to your knee.

- When elongating your legs, ensure that cropped jeans and leggings come to above your knee, at your knee or sit at your ankle. Trousers that come to your midcalf are not flattering on even the leanest of legs!

- When trying to elongate either your legs or your torso, try to stick to simple colours and avoid patterns or too much detail on garments.

## Understanding Patterns and Prints

- On your upper body avoid fluffy materials, fine detail, small floral patterns, and horizontal stripes.

- On your upper body opt for very little detail, soft and flexible fabrics, and horizontal stripes - also avoid shirts and blouses that are not long and a looser straight fit.

- On the lower half of your body you can wear horizontal stripes, patterns, bold prints, bright colours and a variety of materials. Bottoms with a lot of detail, such as combat trousers with pockets, buttons and patterns will help to balance out your body shape.

- Smaller patterns and prints are more likely to make you look fuller than larger patterns and prints will however, both are best to be avoided on "problem areas."

# Idea Looks for Apple Shape - Day, Night and Skirts and Dresses

# Pear shapes

## What is Pear Shape?

Pear shape body shapes (as seen above) are botom-heavy body shapes. They are referred to as "pear shape" because they majority of the weight and width is held at the bottom half of the body, primarily towards the hips, butt and thigh area. Generally, pair shape body shapes have a slim, narrow and leaner upper body and a fuller lower body.

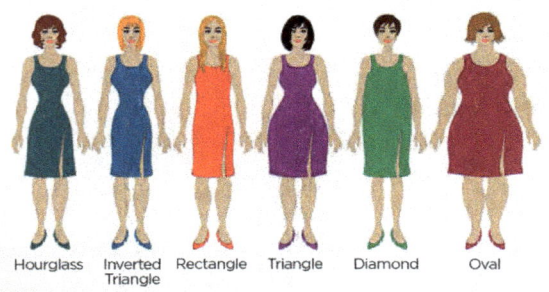

Hourglass — Inverted Triangle — Rectangle — Triangle — Diamond — Oval

## Pear Shape Means:

- Your lower body may be at least one dress size bigger than your upper body
- You are prone to carrying most weight on your hips, thighs and butt.
- You have a narrower upper body and rarely gain weight on your upper body.
- Your waist size is 5 or more inches smaller than your hip measurement.

## Adding Height through Clothing

The main area that you need to focus on if you have a pear shape body shape is the lower half of your body because this is the part that may look the widest and shortest. To elongate your legs, you must:

- Wear trousers that do not have a thick waist band.
- Avoid bottoms made from thick material.
- Avoid trousers such as cords, combats and wide leg trousers.
- Wide leg trousers will make your lower body appear as wide as the width of the trousers, which is why they are best avoided. Instead choose straight leg trousers that skim your legs rather than cling to them. Also, avoid attention grabbing materials, such as lycra, leather, velvet, suede etc.

Choose bottoms with a higher waist line. A decent pair of high waist trousers would be a good idea.

When choosing skirts, an A-line skirt would work better than a pencil skirt.

For cropped leggings and trousers, choose either knee length varieties or ankle length varieties. Avoid cropped leggings that come to your mid-calf because these will make your calves look far wider than they really are and this style is unflattering on all body shapes and sizes.

## Slimming Down a Petite Frame Using Clothing

- Avoid patterned trousers, stick to plainer colours and styles

- Avoid lots of detail on bottoms – i.e. lots of buttons, pockets, zips, etc.

- Keep your bottoms plain and opt for more interesting patterns on top to balance out the difference between your upper and lower body.

- When choosing jeans opt for darker colours or choose a size up or a looser fitting style in lighter jeans such as stonewash and white.

- When choosing jeans, try to find a pair that are dark on the outside of the leg and lighter in the middle. This is like "contouring for legs" – it will shrink the width of your bottom and legs.

Be mindful when choosing back pockets on trousers.

If you want to slim down your derrière then opt for larger back pockets and these will make this area look smaller. On the other hand, if you are trying to fake a larger bottom then go for smaller back pockets.

Avoid thick materials or boxy materials. Choose softer, more moveable fabrics to help prevent further contrast in your body shape.

## Elongating Legs & Torso

- When elongating your legs, ensure that cropped jeans and leggings come to above your knee, at your knee or sit at your ankle. Trousers that come to your midcalf are not flattering on even the leanest of legs!

- When trying to elongate either your legs or your torso, try to stick to simple colours and avoid patterns or too much detail on garments.

- Longer tops that sit slightly below your hipbone will give you a longer looking and slimmer torso. Items such as sleeveless shirts work great for doing this.

## Elongating Legs & Torso

- When elongating your legs, ensure that cropped jeans and leggings come to above your knee, at your knee or sit at your ankle. Trousers that come to your midcalf are not flattering on even the leanest of legs!

- When trying to elongate either your legs or your torso, try to stick to simple colours and avoid patterns or too much detail on garments.

- Longer tops that sit slightly below your hipbone will give you a longer looking and slimmer torso. Items such as sleeveless shirts work great for doing this.

## Idea Looks for Pear Shape - Day, Night and Skirts and Dresses

# Hourglass shapes

## What is Hourglass Shape?

As you will see from the diagram above, an hourglass figure is a body shape that is equal like the banana body shape but with a noticeably smaller waist and a fuller bust and hips. The one main problem that many hourglass shape ladies have is that they need to dress to accentuate their tiny waists if they want to avoid looking as full as their fullest areas (i.e. their bust and butts) all over their bodies.

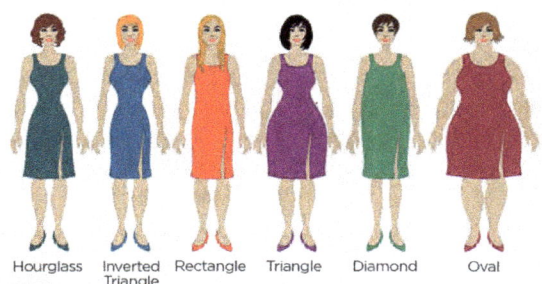

Hourglass   Inverted Triangle   Rectangle   Triangle   Diamond   Oval

## Hourglass Shape Means:

- Your waist is at least 10 inches smaller than your bust and hip measurements

- Your bust and hip measurements are almost equal

- You gain the most weight on your bust, hips, thighs and butt

- You have very small wrists and ankles.

- Your figure appears very balanced.

## Adding Height through Clothing

- Adding a waist belt to highlight where your waist is will elongate your torso and legs.

- Trouser suits, jump suits and high waisted trousers work well in adding height to your particular type of body shape.

# Slimming Down a Petite Frame Using Clothing

- Don't be afraid to dress for your shape and show off your tiny waist and ample curves!

- Due to having a fuller bust, you must accentuate where your bust starts and ends – a good bra is essential. You must also accentuate your waistline in order not to 'shorten' your upper body.

- Wrap tops and dresses will slim down your figure. Remember to wear fitted clothes rather than baggy clothes which can make your figure appear fuller.

- V-neck tops will highlight your hourglass figure in an enviable yet elegant way.

- Avoid round neck tops which will make your proportions appear unbalanced.

## Slimming Down a Petite Frame Using Clothing

- When trying to elongate either your legs or your torso, try to stick to simple colours and avoid patterns or too much detail on garments.

- Wearing high waisted trousers will elongate your legs and emphasise your enviable waist.

- Avoid detail around the hip area, instead (if wearing clothing with detail) make sure that the detail is around the waist area or along the neckline.

- Blazers with long lapels work well in elongating and slimming down your torso, just be sure to find a tailored blazer with long lapels and that sits at least at your hipbone.

## Understanding Patterns and Prints

- Smaller patterns and prints are more likely to make you look fuller than larger patterns and prints however, both are best to be avoided on "problem areas."

- Polka dots, gingham and other traditional patterns look wonderful on hourglass figures.

- Avoid loud prints and slogans, which will make your figure appear fuller without putting any emphasis on your enviable shape.

- Don't be afraid to dress for your shape and show off your tiny waist and ample curves!

## Ideal Looks for Straight Shape

# Straight Shapes

## What is a Straight Body Shape?

There are many names for straight body shapes, including: banana (as shown above), ruler, lean tower, balanced, athletic, celery, and many more. Some of these descriptive words can seem a little intimidating and they can also be a little misleading too. So as to be very clear on what a "straight figure" actually is, we are going to refer to this type of body shape as a straight body shape rather than using any of the above mentioned names.

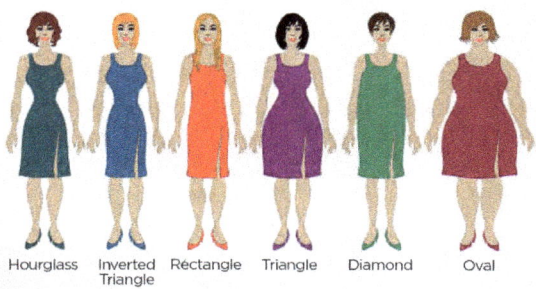

Hourglass  Inverted Triangle  Rectangle  Triangle  Diamond  Oval

Now, although most people with straight figures are usually very slim, having a straight figure doesn't necessarily mean that you are going to have the long, lean figure of a catwalk model. Many athletes, despite being slightly curvaceous because of their muscle, may also have straight body shapes.

## A straight body shape means:

- Your shoulders, waist and hips are all about the same width (with less than 5 inches between them all).

- You do not have any dominant body feature.

- You have slim, equal limbs.

- Generally, your figure is very equal and balanced with no obvious part that is noticeably larger or wider.

- You normally wear the same dress size on both the top and bottom half of your body.

## Adding Height through Clothing

- Usually, you will find that either your legs or your upper body are longer – normally you will find that one area usually appears longer. You can add height to your frame by choosing to accentuate your longer half of your body by wearing an item of clothing that will accentuate the longer half of your body. If it's your legs, then wear a great pair of jeans to show off your long legs, if it's your upper body then wear a tailored fitting short to show off your long, lean torso.

- Stick to straight styles rather than flared styles of garments. Long straight coats, long straight leg trousers and jeans, and straight slim fitting tops will make you appear taller, whereas flared garments, bomber jackets and A-line styles will make you appear shorter.

## Slimming Down a Petite Frame Using Clothing

- If you have a straight figure then chances are that you will gain a little weight all over rather than in one particular area. To slim your figure down you must not focus on one particular area because this can make your body appear out of proportion. Instead choose slim fitting clothing for your upper and lower body. Straight leg jeans that are darker on the outside and lighter in the middle, tops that reach your hip bone and jackets that end slightly below your hips are all a good example of slimming clothing for straight figured petite ladies!

## Elongating Legs & Torso

- The good thing about having an equal/straight body shape is that you can get away with wearing items that other body shapes may not suit. Skinny jeans, shirts, sleeveless shirts are all items that would look great on you and help to elongate certain areas of your body.

- Longer tops that sit slightly below your hipbone will give you a longer looking and slimmer torso. Items such as sleeveless shirts work great for doing this.

- High waisted jeans also look fantastic on balanced, straight figures, as you won't have a muffin top to hang over the waist band of the jeans, making them more flattering. High waisted straight or skinny jeans and trousers will make your legs appear longer and leaner.

- When trying to elongate either your legs or your torso, try to stick to simple colours and avoid patterns or too much detail on garments.

- A peplum hem on a top will give the illusion of wider hips which will also make your upper body and waist area appear narrower, and is an easy way to fake an hourglass figure.

- Choose vertical stripes in clothing for your upper and lower body, as vertical stripes elongate limbs and areas of your body – whereas horizontal stripes do the opposite.

## Ideal Looks for Straight Shape

## Understanding Patterns and Prints

- When you have a straight figure, any pattern and print will suit you. Athletic, balanced and straight figures can even risk mixing bold patterns and prints on both their upper and lower body.

- Fluffy fabrics and woollen garments are excellent materials to wear on your upper body to create the illusion of a fuller looking bust.

- If you want to create fuller looking hips and thighs, patterned leggings, coloured jeans and pencil skirts are the perfect option!

When you have a straight figure, any pattern and print will suit you. Athletic, balanced and straight figures can even risk mixing bold patterns and prints on both their upper and lower body.

High waisted jeans also look fantastic on balanced, straight figures, as you won't have a muffin top to hang over the waist band of the jeans, making them more flattering. High waisted straight or skinny jeans and trousers will make your legs appear longer and leaner.

**CHAPTER 17**

# Size Guide to
## *Petite sizes*

# International Clothing Size Guide

Petite = 5 ft 3 and under

| Euro size | Australia size | UK size | Length (CM) | Circumference (CM) |
|---|---|---|---|---|
| 35 | 1 | 2 | 233.31 | 234.5 |
| 36 | 2 | 3 | 239.98 | 239.0 |
| 37 | 3 | 4 | 246.65 | 243.5 |
| 38 | 4 | 5 | 253.32 | 248.0 |

| UK Sizes (inches) | XS (6) | S (8-10) | M (12-14) | L (16-18) | XL (20-22) | XXL (24-26) |
|---|---|---|---|---|---|---|
| Bust | 33" | 34-35" | 36-37" | $38^{1/2}$-40" | $41^{1/2}$-$43^{1/2}$" | $45^{1/2}$-$47^{1/2}$" |
| Waist | 25" | 26-27" | 28-29" | $30^{1/2}$-32" | $33^{1/2}$-$35^{1/2}$" | $37^{1/2}$-$39^{1/2}$" |
| Hips | 35" | 36-37" | 38-39" | $40^{1/2}$-42" | $43^{1/2}$-$45^{1/2}$" | $47^{1/2}$-$49^{1/2}$" |
| Arm length (petite) | 29" | $29^{1/4}$ - $29^{1/2}$" | $29^{3/4}$ – 30" | $30^{1/4}$ -$30^{1/2}$" | $30^{3/4}$ -$30^{7/8}$" | $33^{7/8}$ -34" |

## International Bra Sizes & Guide

A common issue among ladies with small bone structure is that they require a small band size in their bra but need a larger cup size. For e.g. you may try a bra that's a UK size 34A but find that the band is too large for the size of your back but the cup fits fine. In this case you need to go down a band size and up a cup size – this is a handy trick to know if you do not have the opportunity to go for a professional bra fitting or in the case that a bra you've tried doesn't fit the same way that others in that size do.

Here below is the full list of "petite bra sizes" and their international size equivalents.

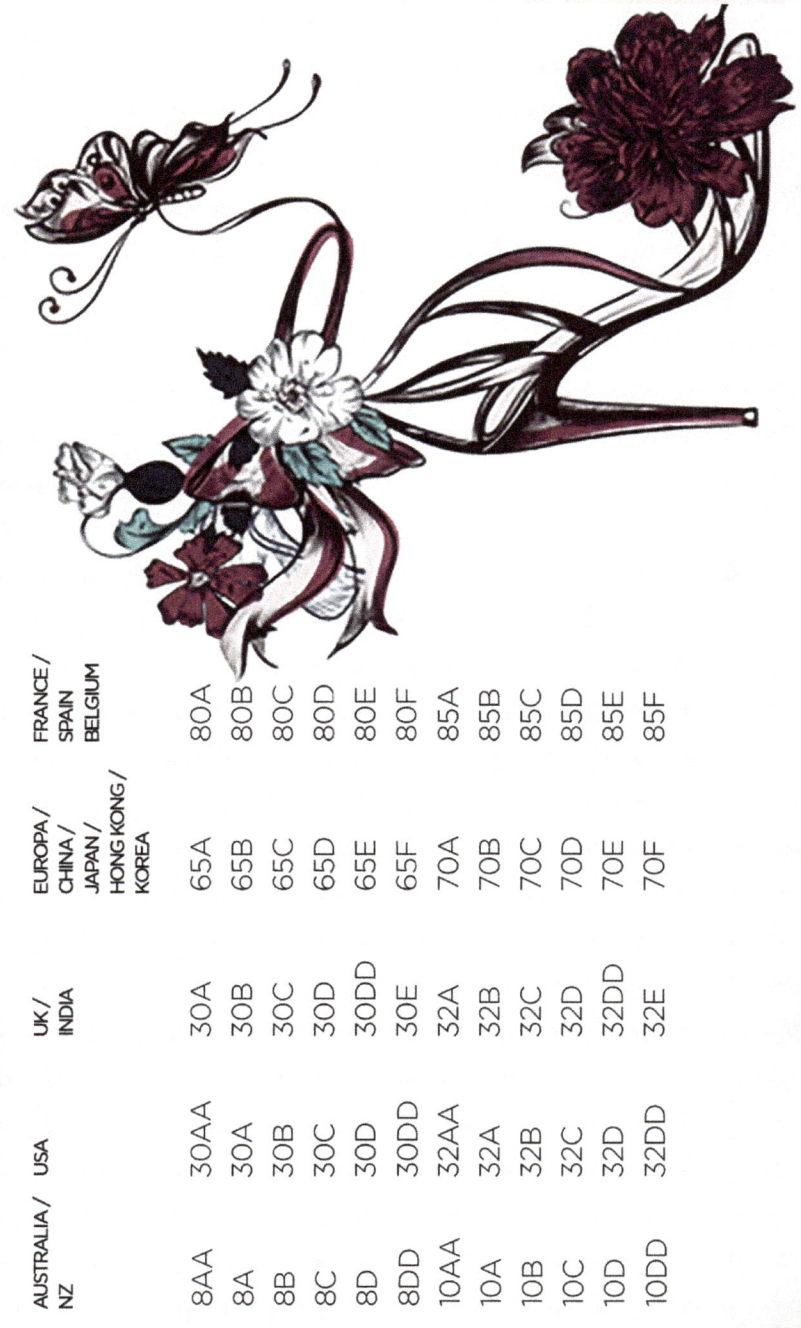

| AUSTRALIA / NZ | USA | UK / INDIA | EUROPA / CHINA / JAPAN / HONG KONG / KOREA | FRANCE / SPAIN / BELGIUM |
|---|---|---|---|---|
| 8AA | 30AA | 30A | 65A | 80A |
| 8A | 30A | 30B | 65B | 80B |
| 8B | 30B | 30C | 65C | 80C |
| 8C | 30C | 30D | 65D | 80D |
| 8D | 30D | 30DD | 65E | 80E |
| 8DD | 30DD | 30E | 65F | 80F |
| 10AA | 32AA | 32A | 70A | 85A |
| 10A | 32A | 32B | 70B | 85B |
| 10B | 32B | 32C | 70C | 85C |
| 10C | 32C | 32D | 70D | 85D |
| 10D | 32D | 32DD | 70E | 85E |
| 10DD | 32DD | 32E | 70F | 85F |

| AUSTRALIA/NZ | USA | UK/INDIA | EUROPA/CHINA/JAPAN/HONG KONG/KOREA | FRANCE/SPAIN/BELGIUM |
| --- | --- | --- | --- | --- |
| 10E | 32DDD/F | 32F | 70G | 85G |
| 10F | 32F | 32G | 70H | 85H |
| 10G | 32G | 32H | 70I | 85I |
| 12AA | 34AA | 34A | 75A | 90A |
| 12A | 34A | 34B | 75B | 90B |
| 12B | 34B | 34C | 75C | 90C |
| 12C | 34C | 34D | 75D | 90D |
| 12D | 34D | 34DD | 75E | 90E |
| 12DD | 34DD | 34E | 75F | 90F |
| 12E | 34DDD/E | 34F | 75G | 90G |
| 12F | 34F | 34G | 75H | 90H |
| 12G | 34G | 34H | 75I | 90I |
| 14A | 36A | 36B | 80B | 95B |

| AUSTRALIA/NZ | USA | UK/INDIA | EUROPA/CHINA/JAPAN/HONG KONG/KOREA | FRANCE/SPAIN/BELGIUM |
| --- | --- | --- | --- | --- |
| 14F | 36F | 36G | 80H | 95H |
| 14G | 36G | 36H | 80I | 95I |

# Measuring Shaft & Heel Height

## Shoe Size Conversion Chart

A combination of Foot Length, Width and Arch comprises a person's exact shoe size.
Example if 2 people have the same foot length but their width and arch is different they WILL wear different size shoes.

| Australia | US | Europe | UK | Asia | China | Foot Length (cm) | Foot Width (Girth) cm | Foot Arch (cm) |
|---|---|---|---|---|---|---|---|---|
| 1 | 2 | 32 | 13 | 210 | 32 | 18-20 | 20 | 21 |
| 2 | 3 | 33 | 1 | 215 | 33 | 19-20 | 21 | 21 |
| 2.5 | 4 | 34 | 1.5 | 220 | 34 | 19-20 | 22 | 23 |
| 3 | 4.5 | 34.5 | 2 | 225 | 34.5 | 21.5 | | |
| 3.5 | 5 | 35 | 2.5 | 230 | 35 | 22.8 | | |
| 4 | 5.5 | 36 | 3 | 235 | 36 | 23.1 | | |
| 4.5 | 6 | 37 | 3.5 | 240 | 37 | 23.5 | | |

## How to find your size

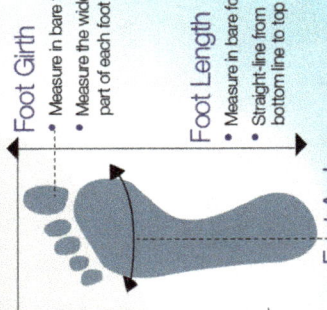

### Components of Petite Peds Shoes

| upper | lining | sole | leather | coatd | textile | other material |

www.petitepeds.com

# Biography

Sharron Halstead is the Founder of Petitepeds, a global online shoe store catering exclusively to ladies with petite feet.

After receiving a multitude of enquiries, comments, complaints, expletives from customers who were fed-up of being treated like second class citizens by the fashion houses, Sharron and her team went about writing "Petite Fashion – The Long and Short of It" to help petite ladies find their own style and sass, and not be at the mercy of a fashion retail world catering primarily to the average size body and foot, but rather use their unique advantage to get the best out of it.

From humble beginnings out of her garage in Melbourne, Australia, she has spread her wings into global markets to assist all petite ladies, the world over, find themselves, their confidence and their self esteem by learning about the basics on how to dress their unique body shapes and petite feet.

*Dear Petite Lady,*

As a thank you for purchasing this book, I'd like to give you a FREE E-Book specifically written to help you on your journey in transforming your Personal Style and Image.

Please visit
http://bit.ly/petitepeds
to claim your FREE Copy TODAY!

# Dear Petite Lady,

hope you enjoyed reading this book as much as I enjoyed putting it together for you. As you can see it is not a book that you read once, but more of a reference library for all things Style for the Petite Lady.

If you enjoyed the book and found it useful, I'd be very grateful if you would post an honest review on our Amazon Page as well as on our Google and Facebook Page.

Your support really does matter and will make a difference, not only to us but also to the countless Petite ladies who want to purchase the book.

I do read all the reviews so I can get your feedback in real time.
Here are the links to leave reviews:

Here are the links to leave reviews:

| | |
|---|---|
| Facebook Review | http://bit.ly/PetitepedsFB |
| Google Review | http://bit.ly/PetitepedsGoogle |
| Amazon Review | http://bit.ly/PetiteFashion1 |

Thank you for your Support!

*Yours fashionably*

**Sharron**
Founder, PetitePeds

www.ingramcontent.com/pod-product-compliance
Lightning Source LLC
Chambersburg PA
CBHW062035290426
44109CB00026B/2632